It's a Special Day!

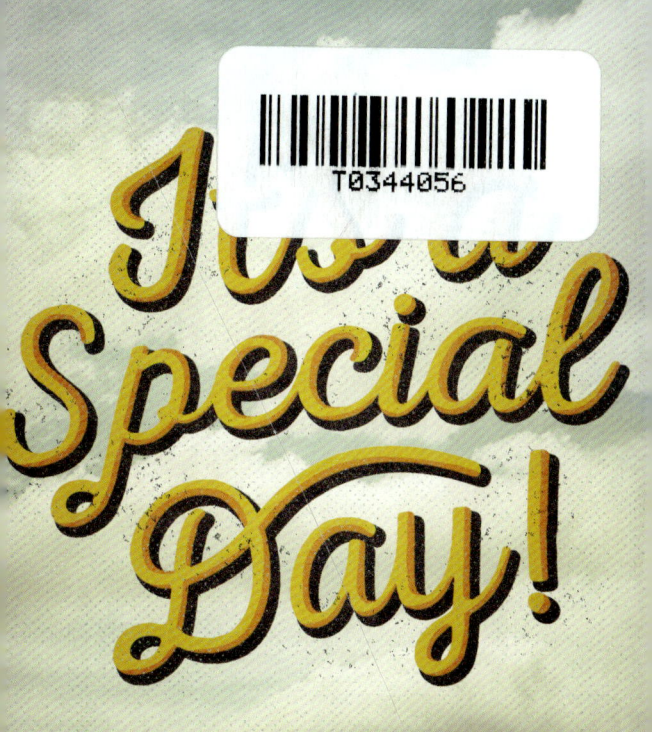

DID YOU KNOW THAT

today is a special day?

It may be an occasion you've been waiting for all year. Or it may seem like just another ordinary day. But whatever is on your schedule, this is God's gift to you—a 24-hour present from your Creator filled with his divine opportunities.

Today, God has opened a new chapter in your life. Yesterday is history. Today is yours now.

So let's celebrate! Let's start enjoying God's goodness now. He delights in showering us with his blessings: "Every good gift and every perfect gift is from above, coming down from the Father of lights" (James 1:17).

Isn't it wonderful that God freely offers us his best gifts to enjoy? Did you know that Jesus is God's ultimate gift to humankind? Without the life, death, and resurrection of God's only Son, we would remain in our sin with no way of escape. God gives us a beautiful creation and the promise of spending eternity with him. But, his richest gift to us is the salvation and grace through his Son, Jesus Christ. Jesus said, "I came that they may have life and have it abundantly" (John 10:10).

Through Jesus, God freely gives us his peace, happiness, and hope both now and forever. If you haven't yet confessed your sin and placed your belief and trust in Jesus for forgiveness, there is no better time than the present. Seek to grow your faith with help from a local Christian church or from a friend who will pray and read the Bible with you. This could be the start of a wonderful new life as a child of God!

On this special day, let's thank God for this gift of life. Let's praise him that he loved us enough to send his Son to free us from our sins. And let's trust him for the days to come.

*This is the day that the L*ORD *has made; let us rejoice and be glad in it.* (Psalm 118:24)

Bible references: ESV.

To be enrolled in a free Bible course and to learn more about Christianity, write to Crossway and include your name, age, and address: **Crossway, 1300 Crescent Street, Wheaton, IL 60187**.

If you'd like to talk with someone about Jesus Christ via text or chat, visit **chataboutjesus.com**.

To read the Bible or find a church in your area, visit **Crossway.org/LearnMore**.

CROSSWAY | GOOD NEWS Tracts

9 781682 163832

www.goodnewstracts.org